GET SET FOR CREATIVE LEARNING SUCCESS

by Imogene Forte

Incentive Publications, Inc.
Nashville, Tennessee

Illustrated by Susan Eaddy
Cover illustration by Francis Huffman
Edited by Susan Oglander
We gratefully acknowledge Ann Conway for her assistance and contributions.

TABLE
OF
CONTENTS

GET SET FOR CREATIVE LEARNING

GET SET FOR ARTS & CRAFTS

GET SET FOR MOVEMENT & MUSIC

GET SET FOR DRAMA & LITERATURE

GET SET FOR CREATIVE LEARNING

The development of the young child's innate creative potential is largely dependent on early environmental influences. Ideally, the arts should be a natural part of everyday life. Music, stories and poetry, the spontaneous expression of feelings and emotions, the opportunity for creative movement, and experiences with color and a variety of art materials can be provided easily and routinely. Often, however, adults responsible for planning and arranging the child's learning environment place far more emphasis on cognitive learning, such as reading and math readiness, than on the affective areas related to creative development. This is partially due to the fact that growth in reading, language, math and science is more measurable, and we can actually "see" what the child is learning.

The child who asks, "What makes the colors in the rainbow?" who exclaims, "Look, the dewdrops on the windowsill look like diamonds with the sun shining on them" or says, "Yellow is my favorite color in the whole world" is demonstrating a creative readiness to explore the wonderful world of color, design and movement and to identify with open-ended artistic experiences. It is at this point that a sensitive adult must take the time to help the child make the most of this magic time for learning.

In addition to encouraging and building upon the child's interests, it is important to set aside time to present projects with specific objectives for creative growth. In order to follow through with a healthy balance of planned and unplanned activities, a good supply of materials, ideas and resources should be collected. This can be done gradually and inexpensively once an overall, open-ended plan is developed.

Good records and beautiful books are expensive, but most public libraries have adequate collections and generous lending policies. Favorite books and records can be identified and placed on the "to buy and keep forever" list. Many libraries also provide paintings and films of selected classics for check-out. A library card in the child's own name and regular trips to the library are absolute musts if at all possible.

An adequate supply of materials for creative exploration can be collected at very little expense. As a matter of fact, many common household items lend themselves to this cause. Food coloring, flour, throw-away containers, seeds, boxes, magazines, gift-wrap paper, yarn — the list goes on and on and is limited only by your imagination. Add crayons, paints, paintbrushes, scissors, pencils and paper, etc.; provide a sturdy storage container; set aside a convenient place to work; and your child will be all set for endless hours of creative self-discovery.

GET SET FOR CREATIVE THINKING

You can help your child develop and use creative thinking skills more easily than you might have thought. With consistent guidance, children can be taught to look and listen, taste and touch, experiment and investigate, and to approach ordinary, everyday things in an extra-ordinary way.

First, the child needs to be helped to acquire and make use of a base of information geared toward his or her learning abilities and intellectual curiosity. It is at this stage that the child needs many meaningful experiences involving the people, places and situations that make up his or her immediate environment. Building and craft projects, group games and discussion, excursions, experiments, good books, carefully selected television programs and pencil and paper activities will provide information and reinforce concepts and skills.

With sensitive nurturing, the child's thinking skills move in a natural progression to the testing level. This is the perfect time for puzzles, mazes, games and individual and group activities to strain the brain, stretch the imagination and challenge logic.

The desirable outcome then, is the stage when the child is ready to experience the joy of his or her own creative potential. Experiences which encourage the child to participate in drama, music, art, creative writing and problem-solving situations become especially important.

Every parent can accompany his or her child along this exciting path of discovery. The ideas, projects and open-ended activity pages that follow are designed to help get you started; some will require a bit of preplanning and organization, but many lend themselves to spontaneous involvement. We hope their use will assist you and your child as you work together toward the development of creative thinking power.

THINGS TO DO
To Get Set For
Creative Thinking

- Take the time to talk with and listen to your child. Ask questions and introduce topics to encourage open-ended answers and provoke follow-up discussion and observation.

- Turn your kitchen into a lab for learning and experiment with a wide variety of materials. Cooking projects and simple science experiments using household equipment and substances are good beginning points.

- Provide lots of good books and make reading a regular part of your family life style. Plan regular trips to the library and read-aloud sessions. Begin with books to fit the child's attention span and increase the complexity of materials as interest levels and listening skills mature. When selecting books, look for creativity and versatility of language usage.

- Write and share letters, lists, stories, poems, songs, slogans, jokes and puns.

- Encourage experiences with creative art materials. Try tempera, finger paints, crayons, charcoal, chalk; butcher, construction, tissue and drawing paper; and anything else you can find.

- Try crafts. Build with wood and nails, sew, knit, macrame, paint, sculpt — all these encourage questioning and brain flexing.

- Develop and enjoy a special family hobby. Change the hobby if you wish, but stick with one long enough to know if it's for you.

- Start a collection. Shells, coins, rocks, wildflowers . . .

- Plan excursions. They don't have to be long or expensive trips — sometimes the walking tour of a neighborhood, park or shopping center, a visit to a nearby farm or factory, or even your own backyard can yield returns in creative learning. Just make sure the trip is planned to meet specific developmental goals and to build pleasant memories of shared experiences.

KITCHEN CAPERS

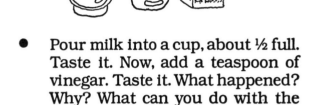

Experiment to find answers to tricky questions...

- Place two ice cubes in an empty glass and two more in a glass with cold water. Which melts first? Why?

- Stretch a wet dishcloth flat on the counter. Tie a second wet dishcloth in a knot. Which one dries faster? Why?

- Cut a potato in half. Place one piece in the refrigerator and one on the kitchen counter. Which one turns brown first? Why?

- Measure up and find out:
  How many teaspoons are in a tablespoon?
  How many tablespoons are in a cup?
  How many cups are in a pint?
  How many pints are in a quart?

- Put heavy whipping cream into a blender or a mixer. Beat and beat and beat. Don't give up — beat some more! Soon you will have two things in your bowl. What are they? (Add salt to the yellow one and put it on your morning toast.)

- Pour milk into a cup, about ½ full. Taste it. Now, add a teaspoon of vinegar. Taste it. What happened? Why? What can you do with the milk now?

- Put some oil and water in a bottle. Shake it. What happens? Do you know why? Now empty the bottle, rinse it out, and put water and soap in it. Shake it. What happens? Why? Finally, empty the bottle, rinse it out and put some salt and water in the bottle. Shake it and see what happens.

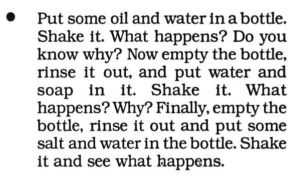

- Peel an onion. What happens to your eyes? Why? Smell your hands. What happens to your hands? Why? Now, wash your hands with salt and water. What happens to your hands? Why?

Cook to learn . . .

 # CHAROSES

1 cup chopped apples

1/4 cup chopped walnuts or pecans

1 teaspoon honey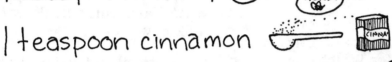

1 teaspoon cinnamon

1-2 teaspoons grape juice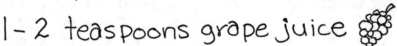

add raisins if you want
    Mix together well and serve

CHUNKY PEANUT BUTTER BALLS

1 cup corn syrup

1 cup chunky peanut butter

6 cups rice cereal

    Combine all ingredients and form "chunks"

on wax paper. The more helping hands

involved the better.

☼ GOOD MORNING MILKSHAKE ☼

1 banana

1 egg

1 teaspoon vanilla

1 cup milk

2 tablespoons apple juice

handful of nuts

Mash the banana with a fork in a mixing bowl. Beat the egg and add it to the banana. Add the milk, juice, vanilla and nuts. Mix well until frothy. Pour into a tall glass and enjoy!

ENGLISH MUFFIN PIZZAS

1 English muffin

2 tablespoons spaghetti or pizza sauce

grated cheese

toppings — hamburger, salami, olives, mushrooms, etc.

Brown the English muffin and add ingredients Pour on sauce Add layer of cheese Broil until bubbly

EXPLORE THE OUTDOORS

- Take a "listening" walk. Close your eyes and listen to all the sounds. Tell someone what you hear.

- Build your own birdhouse. Use a milk carton, a cottage cheese container or a liquid bleach bottle. Attach it to a tree, and wait for your fine-feathered friend to set up housekeeping.

- Find a big rock in a grassy spot. Turn the rock over to find out what plants and animals live underneath.

- Make your own rainbow by standing with your back to the sun and holding a garden hose so that sunlight goes through the spray. Watch closely to see the rainbow colors.

- Be a rockhound. Paint a shiny round rock for a paperweight, glue small stones together to make animals or cover a box or tuna-sized tin can with small pebbles.

- Take a walk to collect pretty leaves. Press some between two pieces of waxed paper (be very careful with the hot iron). Make leaf people or animals. Glue a leaf onto a sheet of paper and use crayons to color on body parts.

- Pick some pretty weeds and arrange them in a jelly jar with a ribbon tied around the top. Give the bouquet to someone who needs cheering up.

- Make mud pies and cakes (not to eat of course) just for the fun of feeling, patting and shaping. Mix the soil with water until it feels all squishy and ready to shape.

- Find a good-sized mud puddle just after a rain. Take an old strainer or colander to dip all the way to the bottom of the puddle. Let the water drain through and see what you have left. Collect enough "puddle findings" (pebbles, sticks, leaves, etc.) to paste on heavy paper for an interesting arrangement.

Draw pictures to show what you think is in the fairy godmother's bag.

Draw a picture to show what you think happened next.

Nessie the sea serpent is fishing for her lunch.
Draw a picture of something you think
Nessie might like to catch.

Sinbad was a sailor
Who sailed upon the sea,
He was a nifty pirate,
And not a kid like me.

If I were a pirate,
I would . . .

Pretend this snowman just came to life.
He needs a new hat and cane, bright shiny eyes and a
   scarf to keep his neck warm.
Can you make them for him?

What is wrong with these pictures?
Color everything except the mistakes.

Use every crayon in your box to fill this jar with jellybeans.
Try to guess how many jellybeans you drew.
Then, count them to see if you were close.

Draw the missing parts for the toys in the Christmas
  stocking.
Add one more toy that you would like to find in your
  Christmas stocking.
Color the toys.

Draw faces to show how the children feel.

21

Make a paper airplane and take it outside on a windy day
    to watch it fly.
Try to figure out why the plane stays in the air.

GET SET FOR
ARTS & CRAFTS

- Make paper bag masks. Be sure to leave yourself nice big holes for breathing.

- Paint with a Q-tip. Dip the Q-tip into liquid tempera paint and make dot patterns on a piece of paper. You can make dot trees, animals, houses, flowers or whatever you choose. Use as many colors as you like, but always with a fresh Q-tip. Just remember, stick to the dots; don't try to paint using strokes — a brush is better for that.

- A robot you're not, but no one will know if you make a box costume (fun for Halloween).

- Make Peanut Butter Balls — you don't even need a stove. Mix 1 cup peanut butter, 1 cup honey, 1 cup dry milk and 1 cup rice cereal together. Shape the dough into small balls and roll in 1 cup coconut. Chill for half an hour before serving.

- Trace your hand or foot on a piece of brown wrapping paper (part of a paper sack will be fine). Then just for fun, paint or draw a face on it.

- Pop popcorn. Watch it pop. What makes it pop? Make popcorn snowpeople. String some for your Christmas tree and don't forget some for the birds.

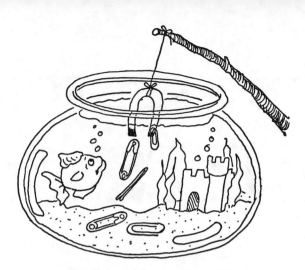

- Save big, thick catalogs to use for pads in art projects. Putting your paper on top of one gives a soft texture for pencil, paint, crayon or chalk projects. When the project is complete, tear off the top sheet of the catalog and throw it away so there is a nice, clean sheet for next time.

- Make potpourri for Aunt Marie or any other nice person. Mix cinnamon sticks, cloves and dried flower petals in a Mason jar and sprinkle with allspice. Leave for a week. Then, put a handful in a net bag and tie with ribbon.

- Bake a monster. Mold cookie dough into the shape of a monster and have a monster party!

- Make your own greeting cards. They are so much more fun than the ones you buy. Use pressed flowers, photographs, pictures cut from magazines, fancy letters and your own drawings.

- Make a puppet from . . .
  . . . an old sock
  . . . a mitten
  . . . a paper bag
  . . . a wooden spoon
  . . . a box

- Design with paints. Put three or four different colors of poster or liquid tempera paint in shallow containers. Use large sheets of paper and objects such as spools, plastic forks, cookie cutters, bottle tops, etc., to make designs.

- Go fishing with a piece of string tied onto a stick. Tie a small magnet onto the other end. Place small metal objects such as paper clips and bobby pins in a fishbowl to be "fished out." If you want to get fancy, you can cut fish out of construction paper and glue the metal objects to the fish.

- Make a "junk sculpture." Collect screws, pipe cleaners, rubber bands, paper clips, pieces of string, old jewelry, toothpicks and other odds and ends to piece together for a one-of-a-kind design.

- Wash a window or two the slow way. Use a cloth to spread glass wax all over the window. Be sure to give it time to dry. Then use your finger to draw anything you choose. Leave it to be admired, then wipe it away with a clean cloth. Shine and polish until the window is squeaky clean.

- Paint with sand — a fine thing to do at the beach. Mix 1 cup sifted, dry, clean, sand and 2 tablespoons powdered tempera. Plan a picture on paper, brush with watered down white glue and shake paint onto glued surface. (If you can't go to the beach, you can always use salt.)

- Make your hand into a puppet. Use a washable marker to draw eyes, nose and mouth. Practice moving and stretching your fingers, one at a time, to make your puppet do all sorts of interesting things.

- String noodles on a piece of yarn to make a necklace or bracelet. If you want a colored necklace, soak the noodles in water with a bit of food coloring, then let them dry.

- While you are into the pasta, sort out some neat, small shapes to glue onto the top and sides of a small box. Let the glue dry and use a Q-tip to dab more glue around the pasta, Sprinkle on gold or silver glitter for a shiny trinket box. You can use shells or tiny pebbles instead to make a great reminder of a special day at the beach or the park. Either of these special boxes will last longer if you brush on a thin coat of shellac.

- Look through old catalogs to find things your family would like for gifts. Cut out just one thing for each person in your family. Give your "make-believe" gifts and find out if you made good selections.

- Bake a cake from a cake mix. Lay a pretty lace doily over the top and sprinkle powdered sugar over it. Gently lift off the doily and the cake will look just like it has been painted with snow by a magic fairy's wand.

- Use every crayon in your box to write your ABC's in living color.

- Cut out strings of hearts or flowers or birds and bees, or anything you please!

- Color lace paper doilies to make fancy placemats for every member of your family. Use different colors to make the designs show up.

- Put homemade finger paint all over a sheet of paper. Instead of using your fingers, use a foam rubber hair roller, an old comb or a plastic picnic fork to make designs.

- Get a great big box and make a house out of it. Paint on windows, cut out a door or make an animal cage, a boat or a barn.

- Choose a nice firm orange to make a sweet smelling ball to hang in your closet. Push cloves into the orange as close together as you can. Tie a pretty ribbon around the orange and make a loop at the top to hang it by.

- Draw or paint a picture of a funny make-believe animal that you would like to have for a pet. Tell a funny story about something that happened to you and your pet.

- Make a bookmark out of a piece of pretty ribbon or brightly colored paper. Write your name on it and place it in your favorite book.

- Take several spice jars and sniff each one. Try to tell someone how the spice in each jar smells to you. Put a little of each spice on your finger and taste it.

- Make crayon rubbings. Lay a leaf, coin or other object with an interesting texture on a flat surface. Cover the object with paper and rub over it with the flat surface of a crayon.

- Use a drinking straw to "blow" a picture. Drop several different colors of liquid paint onto a clean piece of paper. Then, gently blow through the straw. Spread the paint by slowly moving the paper around as you blow to mix the colors. Place the paper flat to dry and you will be surprised to see the interesting design of your finished product.

- Glue a large magazine or calendar picture to a piece of heavy drawing paper or cardboard. Turn the paper over and draw puzzle pieces on the back. Cut the picture puzzle apart. Put the pieces in a box and see how long it takes to put them together again.

- Decorate a plastic strawberry basket by weaving ribbon and yarn in and out of it. Fill the basket with seedpods or wildflowers to make an extra special gift.

- Save all the greeting cards that come to your house. Cut out pretty designs to paste on index cards, old boxes or sheets of writing paper. Write your own happy birthday message. You can save money and give someone a real "made-by-you" greeting.

SOAP BUBBLES

Blow soap bubbles. Mix 1 cup water, 2 teaspoons liquid detergent, ½ teaspoon sugar and 1 teaspoon glycerine. Use immediately.

BAKER'S CLAY

Create a dough picture. Mix ¾ cup flour, ¼ cup salt, water and tempera paint. Add water until mixture is as soft as cookie dough. Add a spoonful of tempera. Use fingers to shape the dough before sticking on the paper.

FINGER PAINT

Fingerpaint with soap suds. Combine ½ cup dry detergent or a capful of liquid soap, and 2 tablespoons liquid starch. Beat with an egg beater until thick. Add food coloring to make different colored paints.

PASTE

Make your own homemade paste and invite a friend to a cut and paste party. Use this recipe: 1 cup water, ½ cup flour, pinch salt. Mix water and flour together slowly in saucepan. Add salt and bring to a boil over low heat. Stir until thick and glossy.

PLAY DOUGH

Make your own homemade play dough. Use this recipe: 1 cup flour, ½ cup salt, 1 cup water, 1 tablespoon cooking oil and 2 teaspoons cream of tartar. Mix and heat ingredients until a ball forms. Add a touch of food coloring if desired.

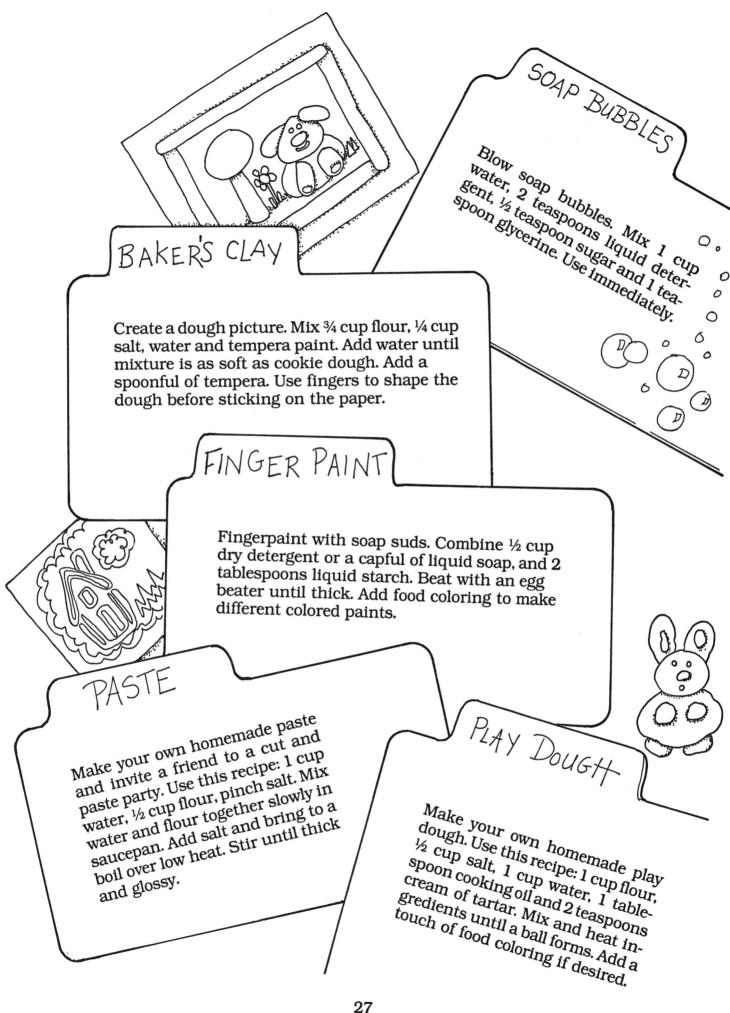

PUPPETS

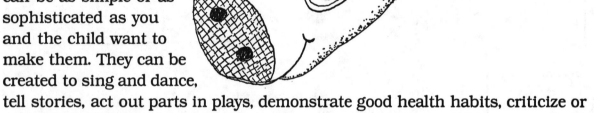

Is it a sock, a sack, a bird or a plane? Making and using puppets of all kinds helps children stretch their imaginations and develop creative self-awareness.

You and your child can make lots of puppets from all kinds of materials, and think up new and creative ways to use them. They can be made from paper bags, socks, mittens, paper cups, construction paper, tongue depressors or even hands or fingers. They can be as simple or as sophisticated as you and the child want to make them. They can be created to sing and dance, tell stories, act out parts in plays, demonstrate good health habits, criticize or give good advice.

Playing with puppets will help the child:
- enjoy vicarious experimentation in social situations
- develop speaking and listening skills
- build self-esteem
- provide interaction with peers
- overcome shyness, self-consciousness
- expose and deal with hidden fears and anxieties
- share personal thoughts and opinions in a non-threatening manner

More importantly, puppets are fun to make and use, and they encourage the child to think and act spontaneously.

Glue ears to back of sack.

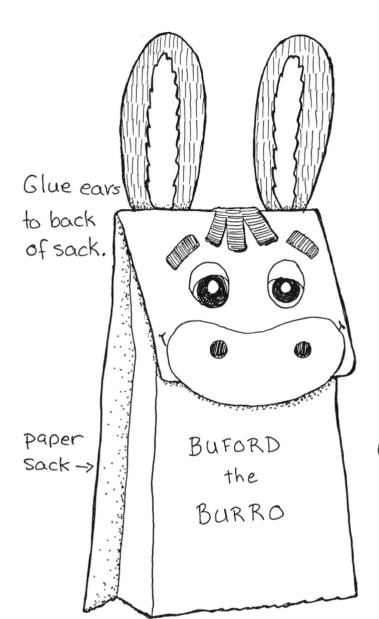

paper sack →

BUFORD the BURRO

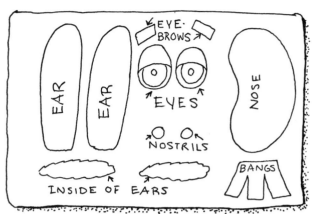

Make features from construction paper. You may use different colors of paper or color the features with markers.

Glue features to sack.

Draw a friend on your thumb.

Use washable markers to draw your puppets.

You can perform behind a table or desk, or even a cut-out sheet of paper.

Draw and cut out a figure from heavy paper. Cut two finger holes and you have a walking finger puppet.

finger holes

Cut off the fingers of an old glove.

Here's another easy finger puppet. Use this pattern and draw any figure in the middle of any type of paper.

tape

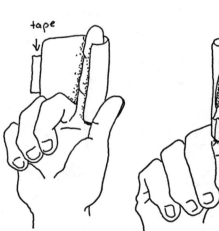

Make a whole handful if you like!

Use a ball point pen or markers to make a fistful of puppet people

Wrap paper around finger and tape together.

Attach construction paper ears with glue.

Use markers to draw a face for a balloon bunny.

Draw and cut out a figure from heavy paper.

Tape or glue construction paper features to an empty cardboard tube.

Glue to a popsicle stick and you have a rod puppet.

Tape a stick to the inside and your puppet is complete.

31

Cut wings from construction paper and glue to back of bag.

Draw face and hair on white paper. Color, cut out and glue to bag.

paper bag

TO MOMMY FROM JOY

Use crayons or markers to draw dress, arms, and legs.

An old fuzzy sock makes a friendly puppet puppy.

Curl fringed paper around a pencil for eyelashes.

Use an old dog collar, or make one out of paper.

Glue on felt or cloth for ears.

Make other features from felt or paper.

32

Here are three circles.
Use your crayons to make each circle into something different.

How does your garden grow?
Draw plants to make a vegetable garden, a flower garden or even a magic garden.
Color the plants and make up a story about the garden.

Draw a picture of something . . .

ugly

tiny

lovely

scary

Draw a picture to show each person described below.

A happy teacher

An angry boy

GET SET FOR
MOVEMENT & MUSIC

- Maybe you can't go to Hawaii this winter, but you sure can make yourself a hula skirt from fringed crepe paper. Then, make up your own hula dance and perform it for a group.

- Sing wherever you go just to hear the sound of your voice — yodel, hum and whistle, too. Learn the words and tunes to some of your favorite songs.

- Be a tightrope walker. Lay a jump rope in a straight line on the floor. Try to walk on the rope without getting either foot off. Then try to walk on a wavy line, a circle and a figure eight.

- Make up a sleepytime lullaby to sing to your favorite doll or teddy (or if you have a little brother or sister, that's even better).

- Pretend you are the chief of a proud Indian tribe. Make up a dance for a special celebration.

- Try to move two parts of your body to do two different things at the same time. (Draw on a piece of paper while you are moving your foot in a circle, or wave your arm over your head while you wink your eye.) It's harder than you think.

- Did you know that you can use your own body as a rhythm instrument? Try making rhythmic sounds by clapping your hands, slapping your knees or snapping your fingers. Stand and use your feet to slide, stomp and tap!

- Sit on the floor and try to curl up like a ball. Feel and act as round as you can and roll around just like a ball.

- Dance a scarf dance. Hold up a long silk scarf, dip and twirl — where the scarf goes, you go — gracefully, please!

- Listen to the record "Peter and the Wolf" (Leonard Bernstein and the New York Philharmonic, Columbia Records). Just listen the first time, then act out the story.

- Sing action songs and act them out. Good ones to begin with are:
  "I'm a Little Teapot"
  "Ten Little Indians"
  "Where Is Thumbkin?"

- Fingerpaint to music. Move your fingers as you "feel" the music. Try —
  "The Surprise Symphony"
  "The William Tell Overture"
  "Swan Lake"

CREATIVE BODY TALK

Sometimes, actions speak louder than words.
Use your body to tell someone . . .

goodbye

move over

go away

come closer

Use your body to show . . .

. . . an elephant swinging her trunk

. . . a snake slithering along the ground

. . . a race car in an important race

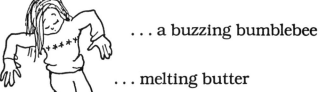

. . . a buzzing bumblebee

. . . melting butter

. . . an egg beater

. . . a lawn mower

. . . a pancake on a plate

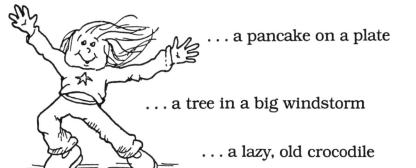

. . . a tree in a big windstorm

. . . a lazy, old crocodile

. . . a ball being bounced

Use just your hands and arms to show how you would . . .

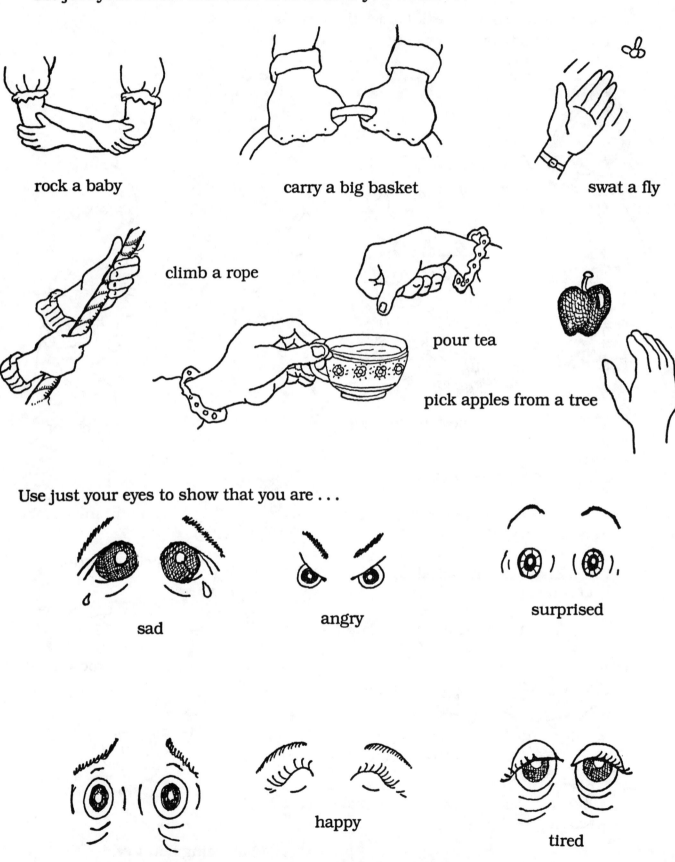

rock a baby

carry a big basket

swat a fly

climb a rope

pour tea

pick apples from a tree

Use just your eyes to show that you are . . .

sad

angry

surprised

frightened

happy

tired

40

Start with A and end with Z,
Pretend to be each letter you see.

GET SET FOR
DRAMA & LITERATURE

- Draw three faces. Make one face happy, one sad and one angry. Make up a story about the three faces and tell why each one shows that feeling.

- Read some of your favorite nursery rhymes. Tell how you think the people in the nursery rhymes looked, how they felt and what happened to them. (How old was Little Boy Blue? Was he brave or timid? Did he blow the horn in time or did he get in trouble?) How about Little Jack Horner, Old Mother Hubbard or Little Miss Muffet, etc.?

- Use blocks, toy cars and trucks, plastic animals and whatever you have in your toy box to build a make-believe town. Give your town a name, and make up a story about what goes on there.

- Paint the biggest truck you can paint on the biggest sheet of paper you have. Make up a story about the truck — where it will go, what it will carry and who will be driving.

- Pretend you are in a hot air balloon floating over your own house. Tell a story about who and what you can see when you look down.

- Pretend someone gave you a pet dinosaur for a birthday present. Tell what you would name it, feed it, where it would sleep and what you would tell the neighbors.

- Find a picture in a magazine or a library book that shows people doing something (a family at the dinner table, a birthday party, people in a car, etc.). Make up a story to tell what will happen next.

- Save empty cereal boxes, coffee tins, etc., to set up a store. Put prices on your make-believe items and play storekeeper with whomever will come to buy from you.

- Choose a hat for a day from a big box of hats. Select one you would like to wear to be somebody different. Put the hat on, try to think like that person and act out the role.

- Play the "I see" game with three, four or more people. The first person says "I see something you don't see and it rhymes with groom." (Be sure the object is in plain view.) The person who guesses the right object, gets to name an object next. Colors or beginning sounds may be used instead of rhyming words.

- Find yourself a silly-time tree — one you can sit under, climb or jump and skip around. Use this tree when you really feel silly. Tell silly stories, corny jokes, nonsense rhymes, riddles, or pretend to be crazy characters — always under your silly tree and with people who want to be silly just like you do!

- Move some chairs together to make a bus or train. You be the driver and "hit the road."

- Try to show different feelings just by walking — walk happily, proudly, fearfully, bravely. Add some walks of your own.

- Make your own book. Try . . .
  . . . a construction paper cover
  . . . a brand new notebook with a solid-colored cover that you can design yourself
  . . . a scrapbook about a trip
  . . . a "me" book for Grandma or Aunt Lucy

- Make up a funny story about a piggy bank that comes to life.

- Make your own collection of dress-up clothes — the fancier the better. Add lots of hats, shoes and jewelry (wigs are lots of fun if you can get some).

- Pantomime is fun — it is acting out experiences without any words. Pantomime:
  — unwrapping a lollypop, throwing the paper away, licking the lollypop, then throwing away the stick.
  — picking up a tiny baby, putting it in its crib, patting it on the back and pulling the blanket up.
  — taking a package from the mailman, opening it, taking the present out, looking at it, then putting it back in the box.

- Think about what you want to be when you grow up — butcher, baker, police officer, teacher, doctor, lawyer, nurse or chief — act out the part and have someone guess what your job is.

- Cover a card table with an old sheet or tablecloth to make a hideaway. It can become a cave, a desert island, a tunnel or just your own special thinking place.

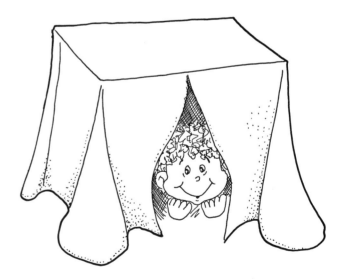

- Get your own library card. Visit the library as often as you can and check out books about things to know and things to do, and most important of all, books that will be just fun for you!

- "Read" and talk about one of these beautiful picture books.
  - **Gilberto and the Wind** by Marie Hall Ets
  - **Andy and the Lion** by James Daugherty
  - **Millions of Cats** by Wanda Gag

- Make up a story about:
  "The Little Witch Who Got Lost on Halloween"
  "The Easter Bunny Who Didn't Like To Hide Eggs"
  "Santa's Reindeer Who Hated Cold Weather"
  "The Heart That Fell Apart"
  "The Leprechaun Who Grew into a Giant"
  "The Dreidel That Couldn't Stop Spinning"

- Sing and act out the song "Here We Go 'Round the Mulberry Bush" by changing the words and actions to show some of the things you like to do.

  "Here we go 'round the Mulberry
      Bush, The Mulberry Bush,
      the Mulberry Bush,
      Here we go 'round the
          Mulberry Bush,
  So early in the morning."

  This is the way I ride my trike...
      ...walk to school
      ...read my book

- Make these sounds and then act them out...
      ...a zipper zipping
      ...a motor roaring
      ...rain falling on a rooftop
  Make up some more noises and ask someone else to act them out for you.

- Make up rhymes with rhyming words. It gets easier as you practice. Here are some words to use to get you started:

and	**bat**	**call**	**well**
band	cat	fall	bell
hand	fat	tall	tell
sand	hat	ball	sell
land	rat	wall	fell

ring	**me**	**fist**	**go**
king	be	list	no
sing	we	mist	so

book	**night**	**broom**	**day**
cook	fight	zoom	hay
took	light	loom	lay
hook	sight	doom	say
look	right	room	may

bar	**bed**	**ten**	**gold**
far	red	hen	cold
jar	led	men	sold
tar	fed	pen	told

- Make up a TV commercial for your favorite food. Pretend you are on the air and present the commercial to your viewers.

- Pretend you are ...

    ...a spaceship blasting off
    ...a goldfish in a fish bowl
    ...an old truck on a country road
    ...a kite in the sky on a windy day
    ...Humpty Dumpty falling off the wall
    ...a turtle sticking his head out of his shell

MAKE UP STORIES TO FINISH . . .

You can help your child to develop the visualization and inference skills so important to creative thinking by asking him to supply endings for stories that you make up.

An added bonus of this type of activity is the comradeship and good feeling that comes as an adult and child share the spontaneity and excitement of a "first-time-ever" story ending. Special favorites may be told over and over, with the same ending or a different ending each time. The stories also may be used to develop mental imagery skills by asking the child questions. This provides opportunities to describe people, places or things as the child sees them, and to add to and take from settings, plots and sequences.

Providing paper and art supplies to illustrate favorite stories will also help the child to creatively internalize the experience. Encourage the use of more than one art medium when possible. Drawing or coloring with felt tip pens or crayons is fine, but young children can express ideas equally well through torn paper collages, paints, cardboard box dioramas or cut-and-paste activities.

Tell happy stories, sad stories, silly stories and what-would-you-do stories. Use fun and fantasy, fact and real-life situations and as many different plots, casts of characters and settings as your imagination allows. Here are a half-dozen to get you started!

Zimron sat in his spaceship waiting for permission to take off. Everything was in order. He and his crew had practiced for weeks getting ready for this mission. Now, he was a little nervous. After all, this was the first time he had left his home planet. Blastoff! Zimron is off to find new planets and maybe new beings. After several weeks of searching, he and his crew land on an unknown planet. It is covered with large, soft bush-like objects. Zimron wonders if you can eat them. All of a sudden, one of the strange, soft objects . . .

Dinky Dinosaur woke up to find himself all alone in the forest. Last night, his mother, Donna Dinosaur, had tucked him in and read a bedtime story to him. Just before he fell asleep, his father, Danny Dinosaur, had stuck his head around the big tree to tell him good night. This morning, both his parents were gone. The forest seemed unusually quiet. Suddenly, Dinky heard . . .

Sally was always playing silly tricks on her brother. She would climb into the top bunk of their bunk beds and pretend to be sleeping. She would put some of the dog's food on her brother's plate at breakfast. Then, one day she decided to . . .

The students at Heather's school could bring their favorite toy to Toy Day. Heather was afraid her favorite doll would get dirty or broken, but she wanted to take the doll to school to show her friends. She decided to . . .

Misty always wanted a puppy of her own. Her father said maybe next year when she was older she could have one. But, Misty wanted a puppy NOW. She thought and thought about how she could get a puppy this year. Suddenly, an idea came to her. She said, "I know how I can get a puppy! I can . . . "

Every afternoon, at exactly four-thirty, Hank finished his chores and went out to play with the guys. Today was the same kind of day, so he finished feeding the dog, getting his homework done and setting the table for Mom. But, when he went outside, it was not the same kind of day. Everything was a different color. The flowers were sparkling gold and silver, the grass was a bright, bright blue and the sky was orange! The most unusual sight of all was the unicorn at the bottom of his back steps. The unicorn told Hank he had come to take him far away to a magical land. Hank climbed on the unicorn's back and flew through the air with the clouds floating in front of them. All at once, Hank saw before him the most magical land of all, everything was . . .

Draw two chickens.
Make up a funny story about the chickens.

The March wind blows,
It cools our toes.
Where is it going
All the time it is blowing?

Make up a story about something you would like to do
on a windy day.

Peter, Peter,
    pumpkin eater,
Had a wife, and
    couldn't keep her.
He put her in a
    pumpkin shell
And there he kept
    her very well.

Draw a picture to show what you
would keep in a pumpkin shell.

Little Boy Blue,
Come blow your horn,
The sheep's in the meadow,
The cow's in the corn.

Where is the boy
Who looks after the sheep?
He's under the haystack
Fast asleep.

Draw a picture to show what Little Boy Blue is dreaming of.

Here are the pickle people.
Make one grumpy and grouchy.
Give one a twinkle in his eye.
Let the last one be bashful and shy.
Now, tell a story about these characters.

Ask a grownup to help you write the names or draw pictures
of your 3 favorite books.
Make a red star beside the one you like best of all.

Gorilla Tales

Finish drawing this truck.
Color the truck.
Make up a funny story about something that happened
   to the truck.

Draw dot-to-dot.
Make up a story about the kangaroo.

Find and color all 26 letters of the alphabet.

Poor Porky may be in real trouble this time.
Use your crayons to trace his trail and color the picture.
Then, tell his tale.

HAV-A-HART TRAP

PORKY PINE

Tell the story these pictures show.
Color the pictures.

Look carefully at this house.

Use blue, black and brown to color the picture.

Tell how you would feel, what you would do and who you
would like to have with you if you had to spend a night
in this house.

Help Nora clean out her sewing basket.
Mark out the item in each group that does not belong
   in a sewing basket.
Color the other items.

Tell what is happening in each picture.
Color the pictures.

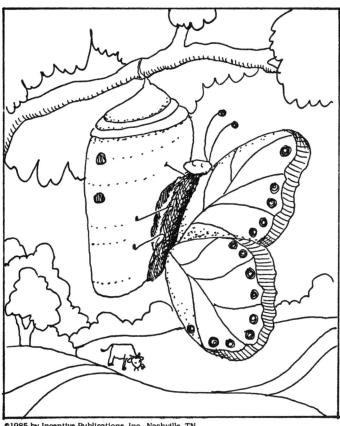